My Country

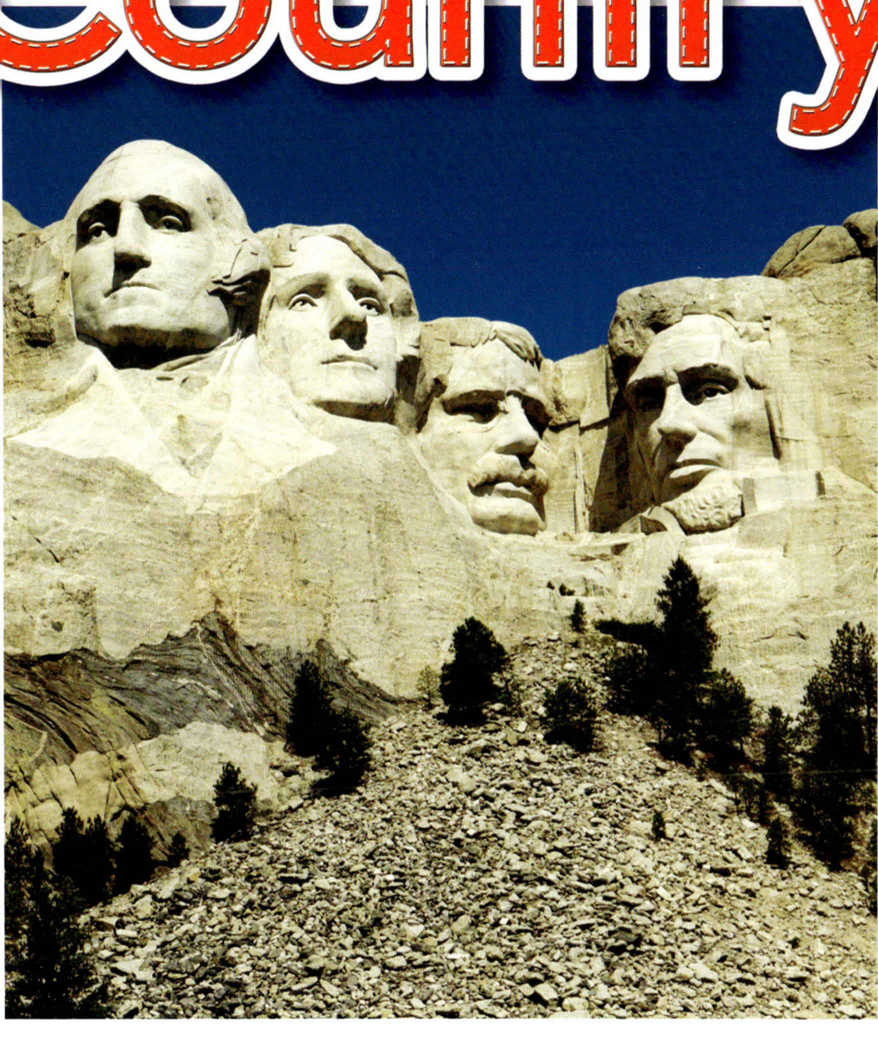

Stephanie Reid

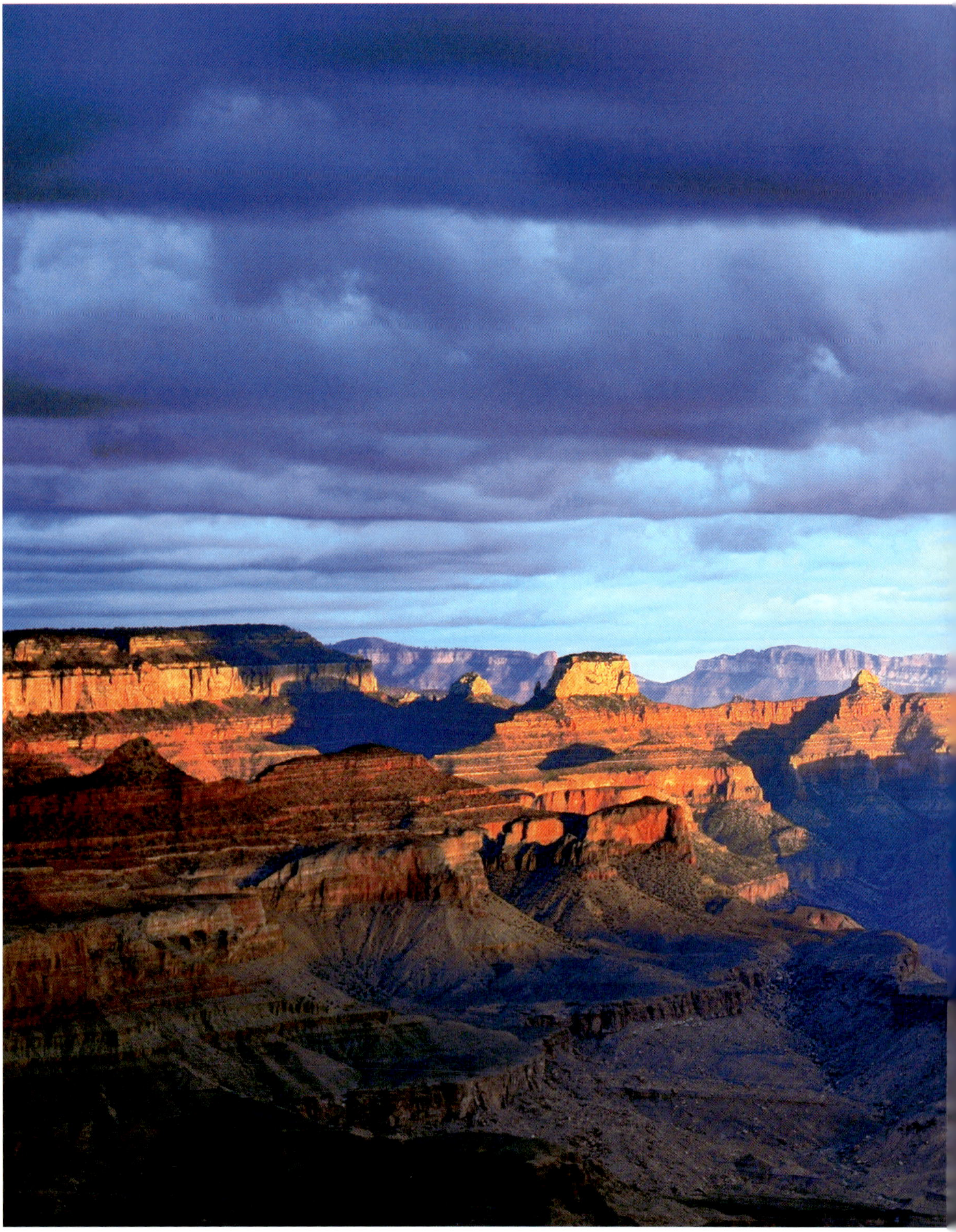

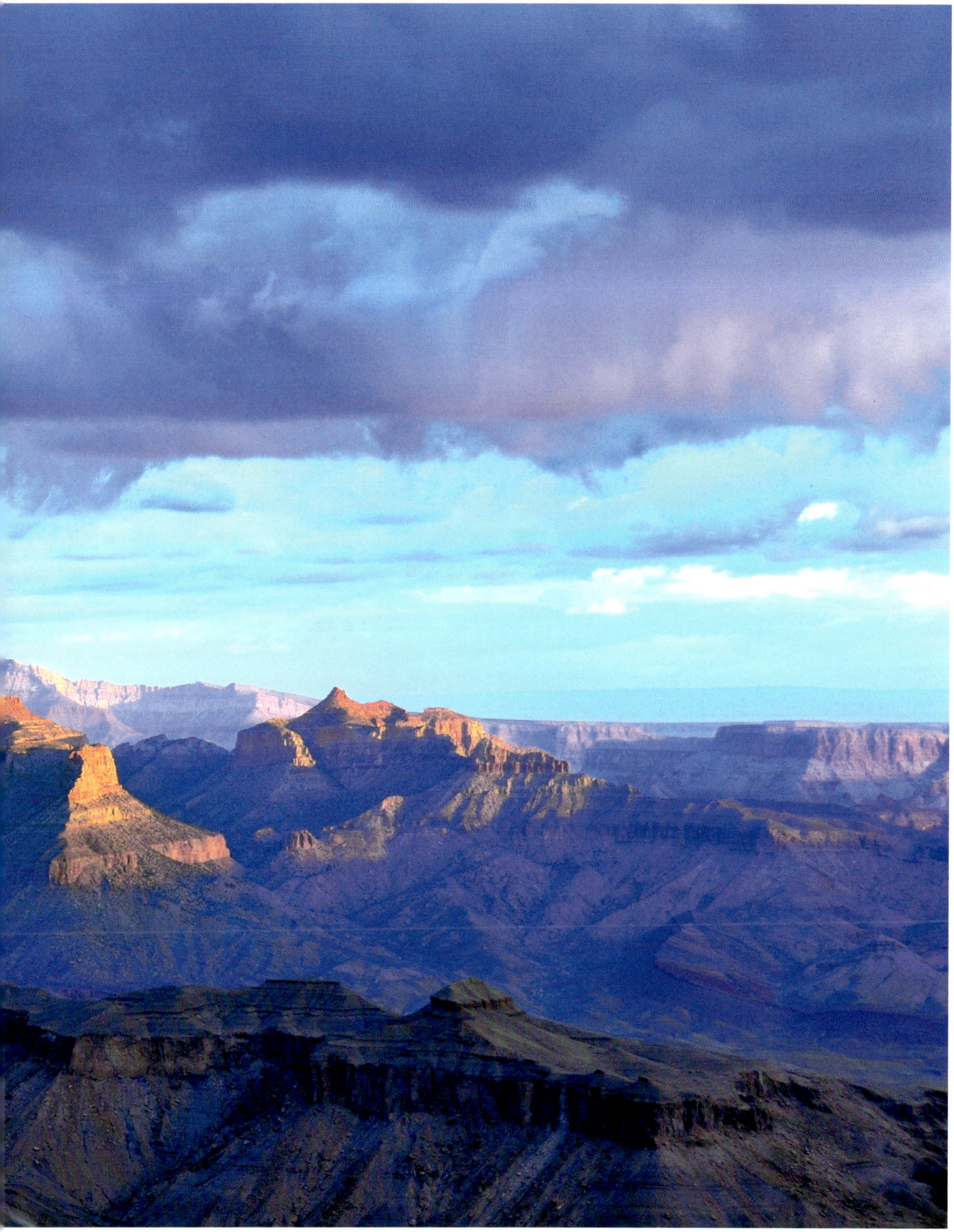

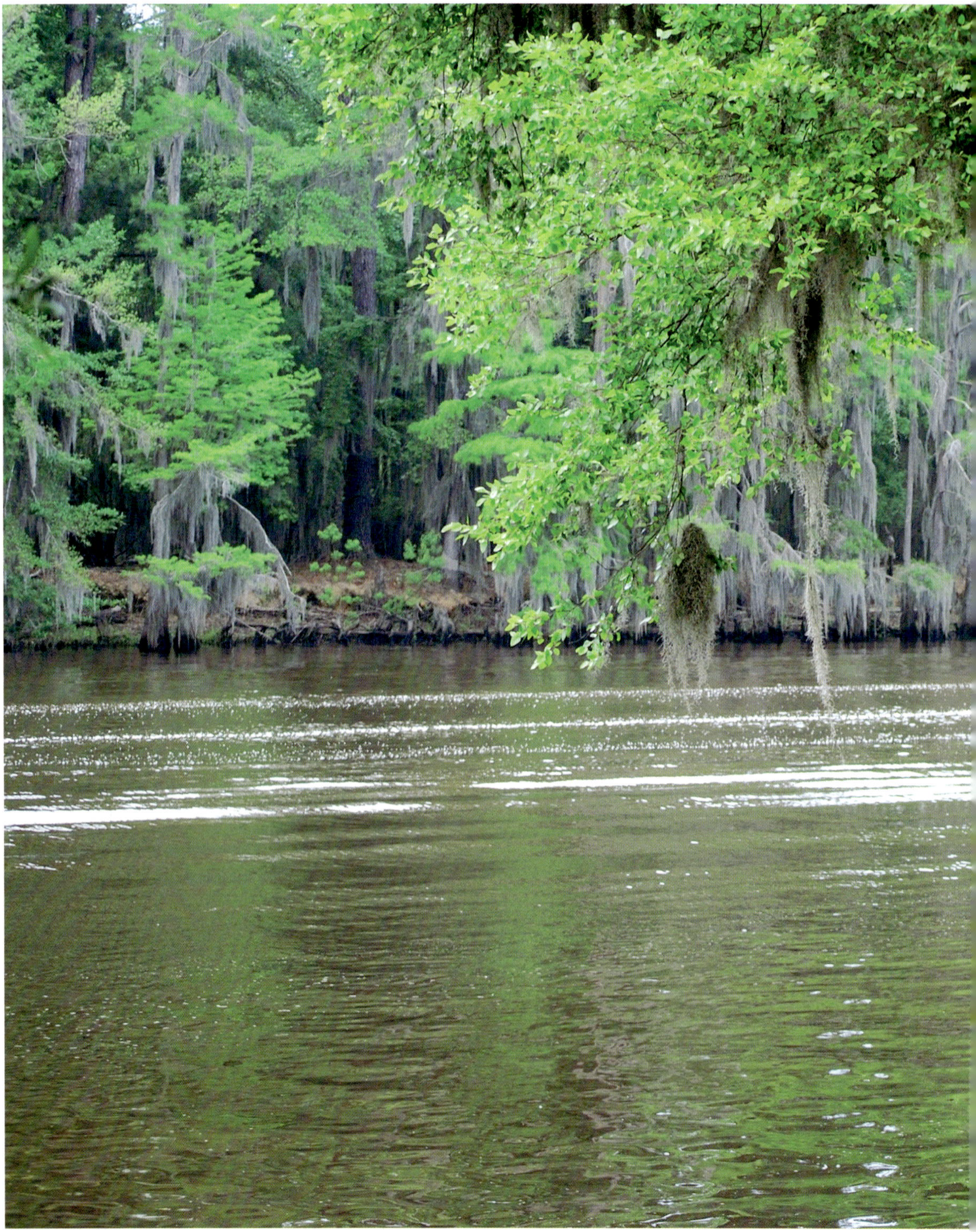

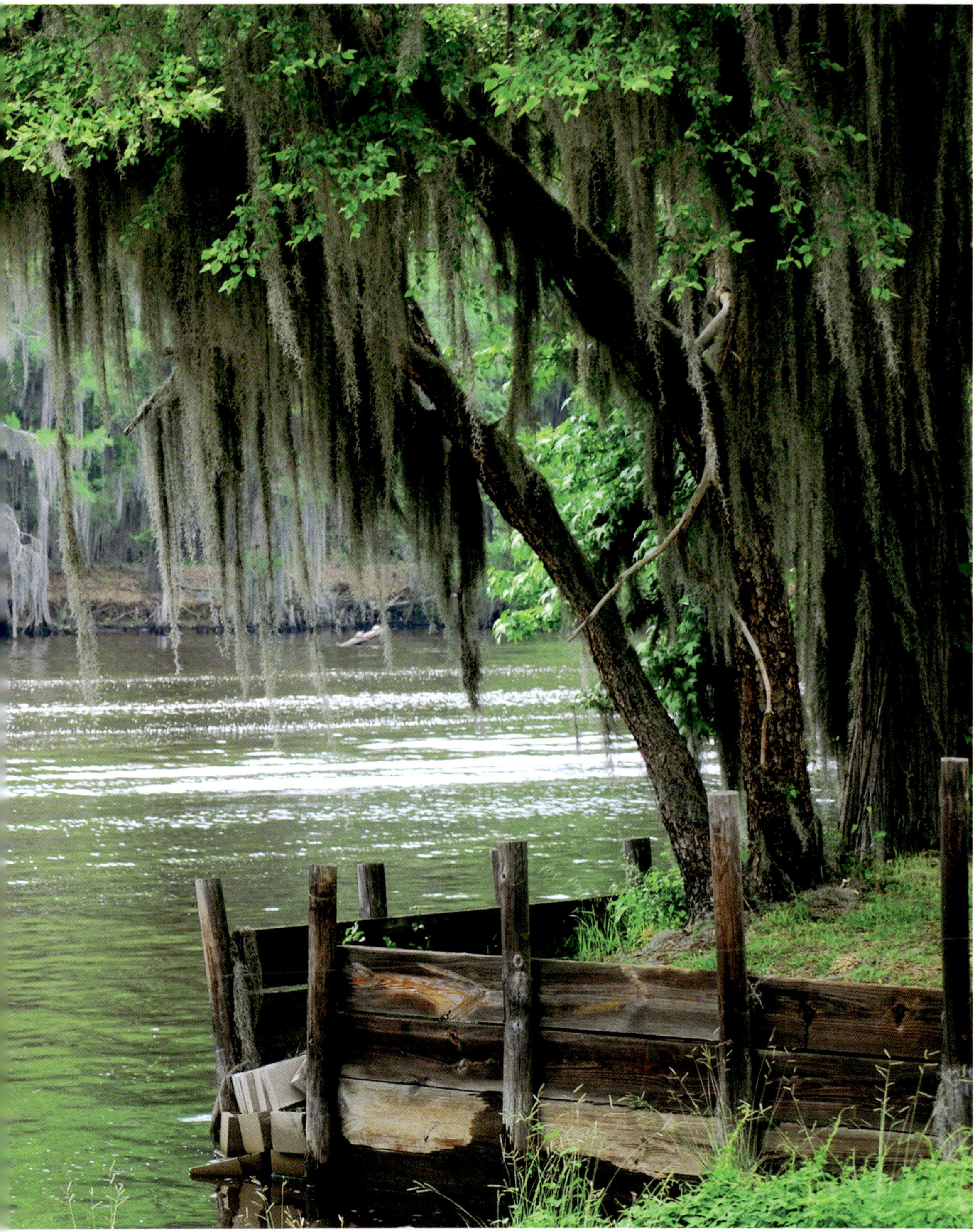

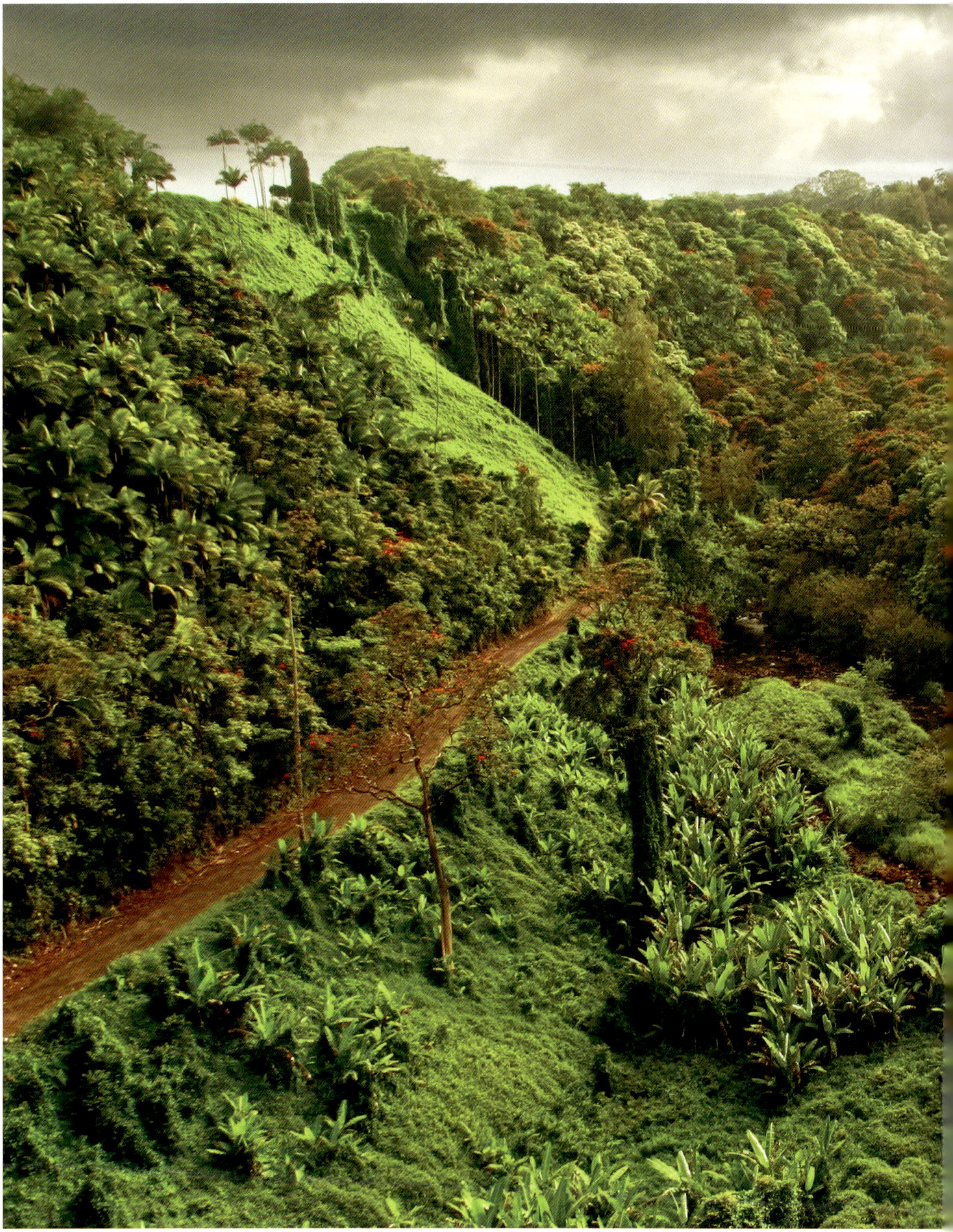

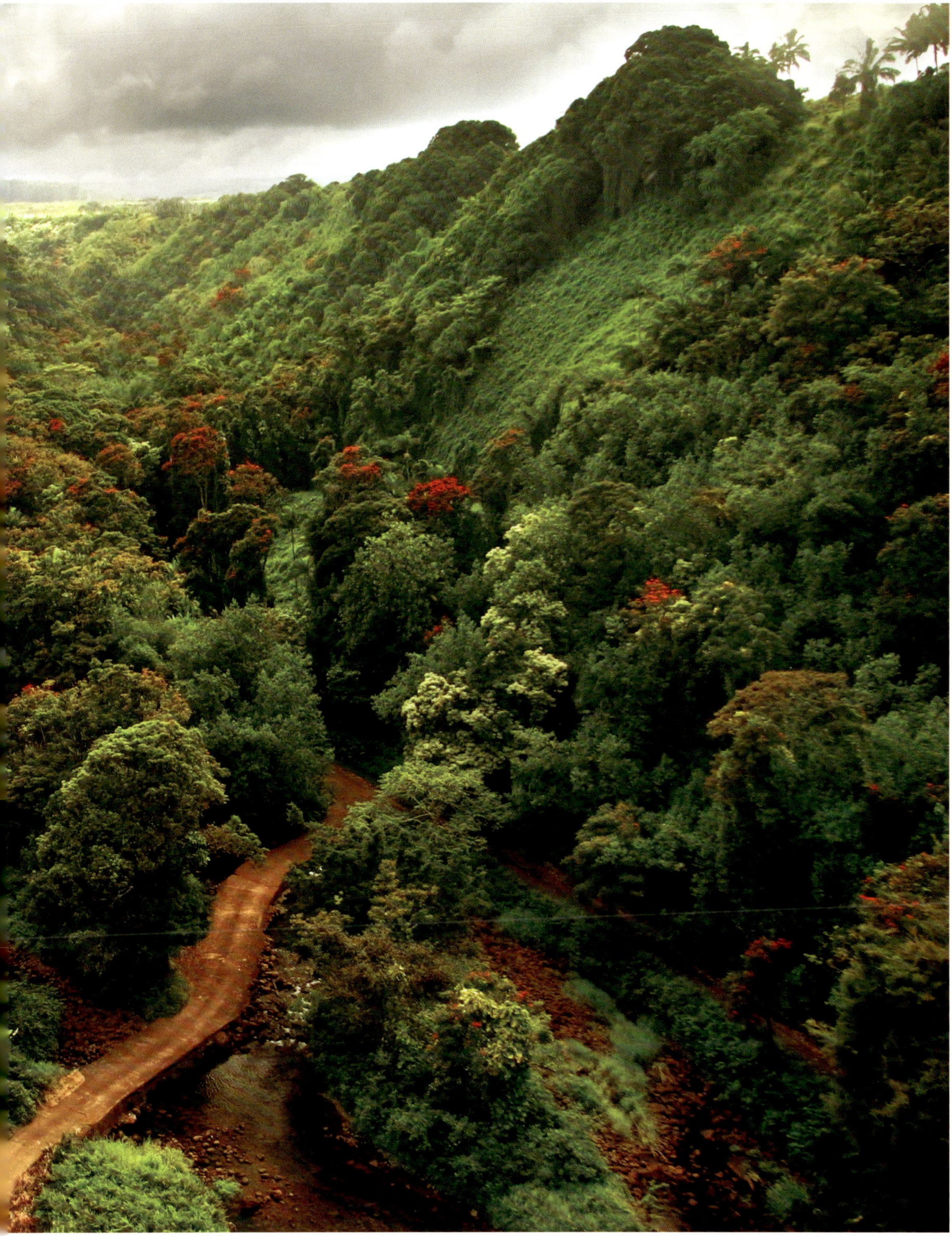

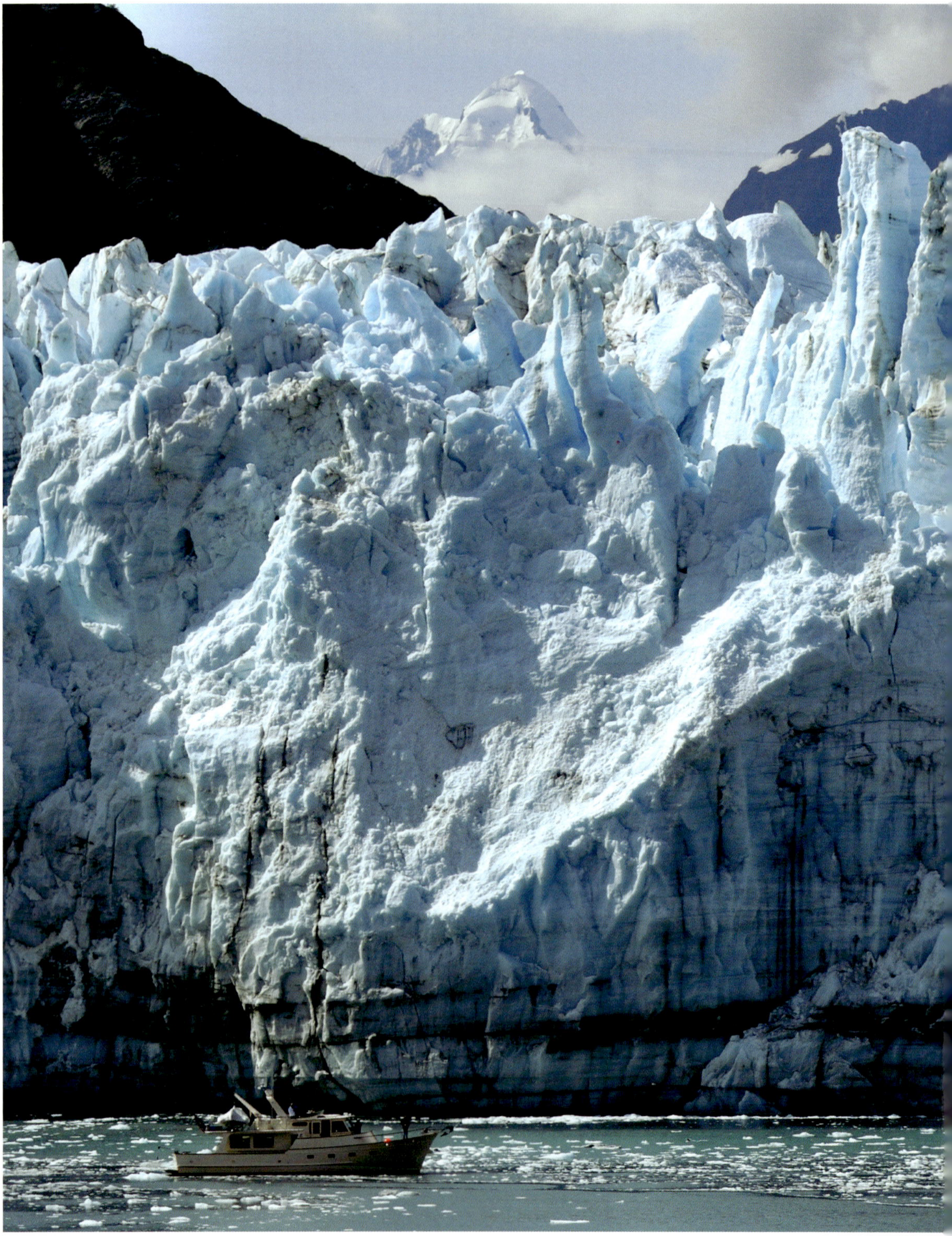

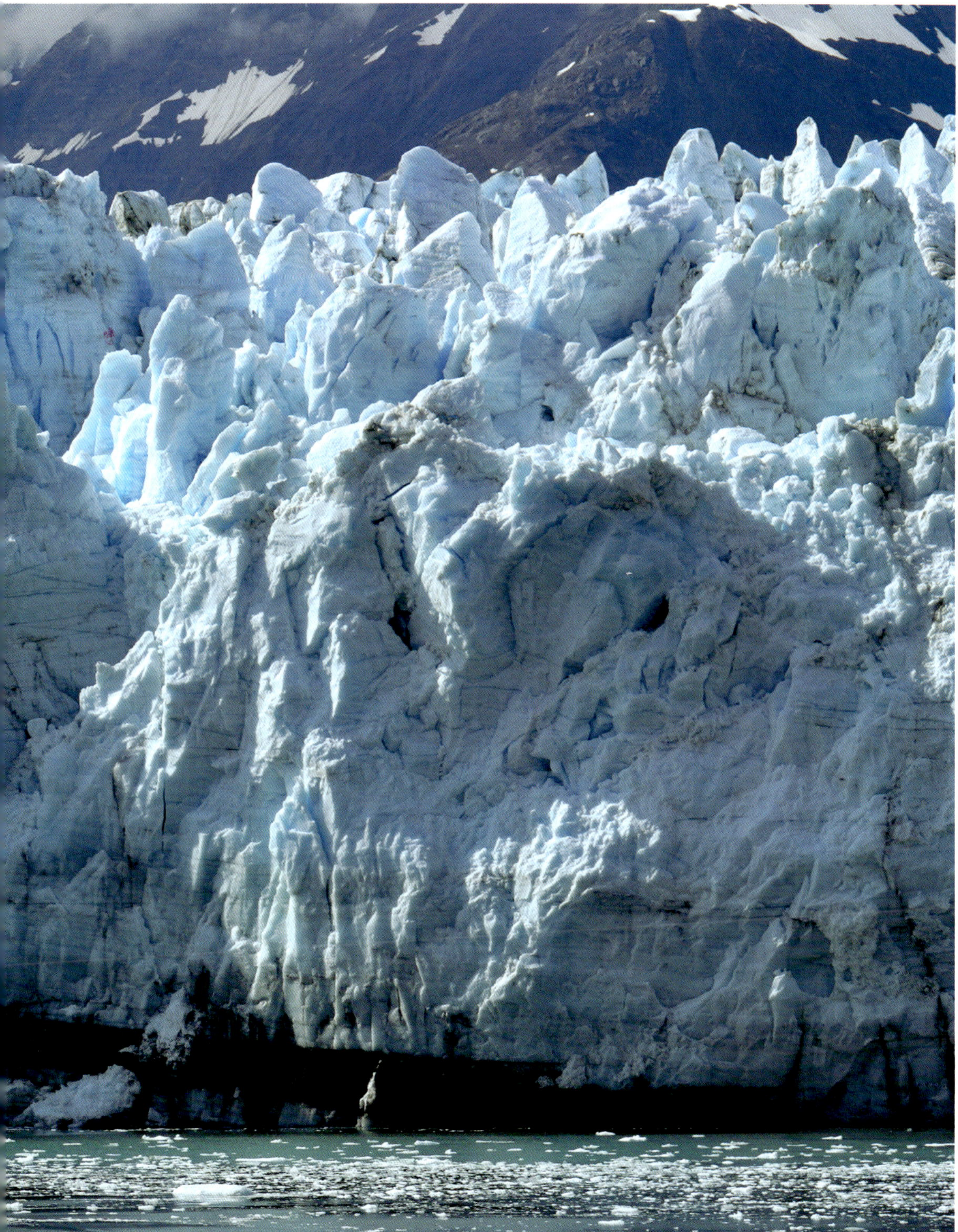

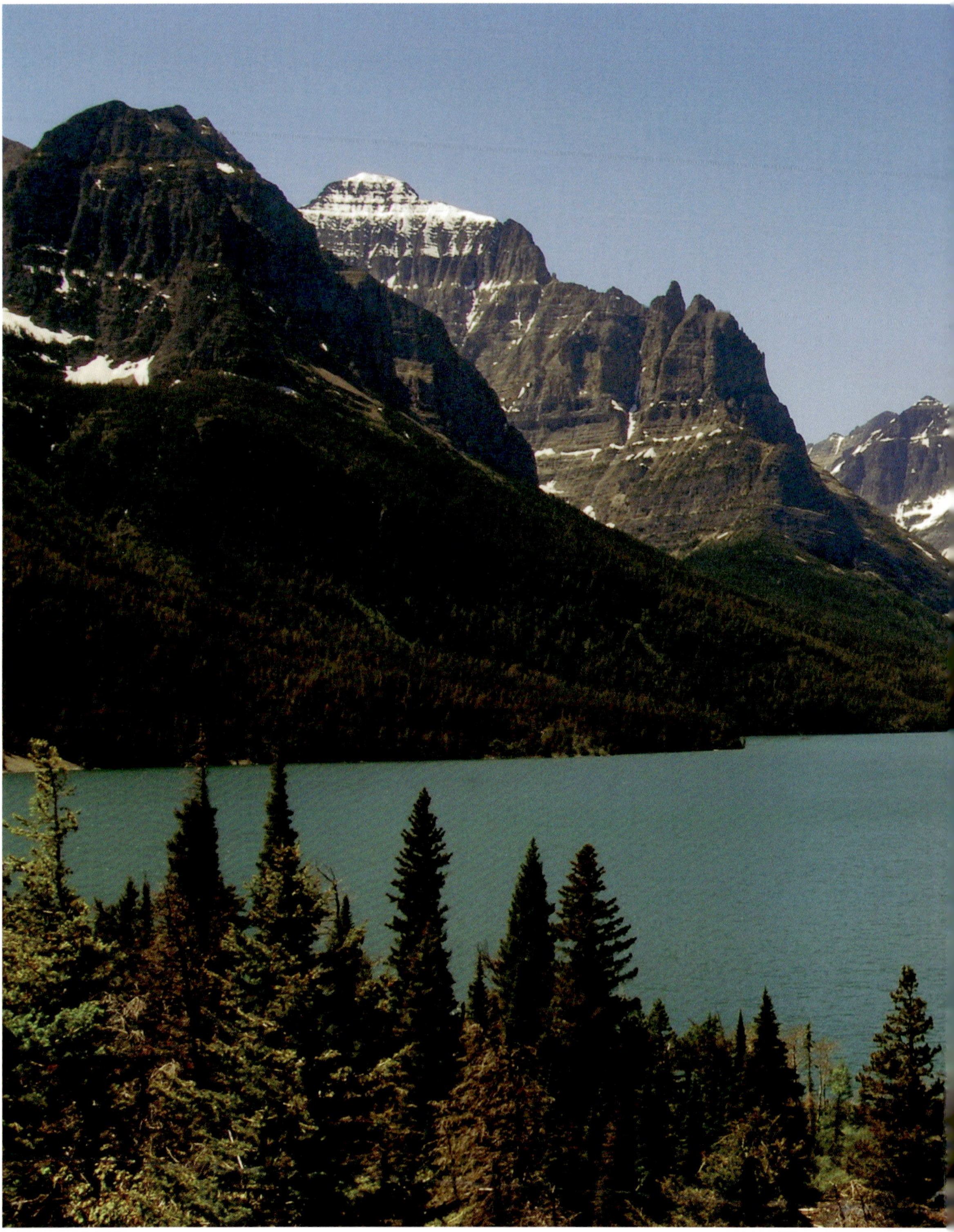

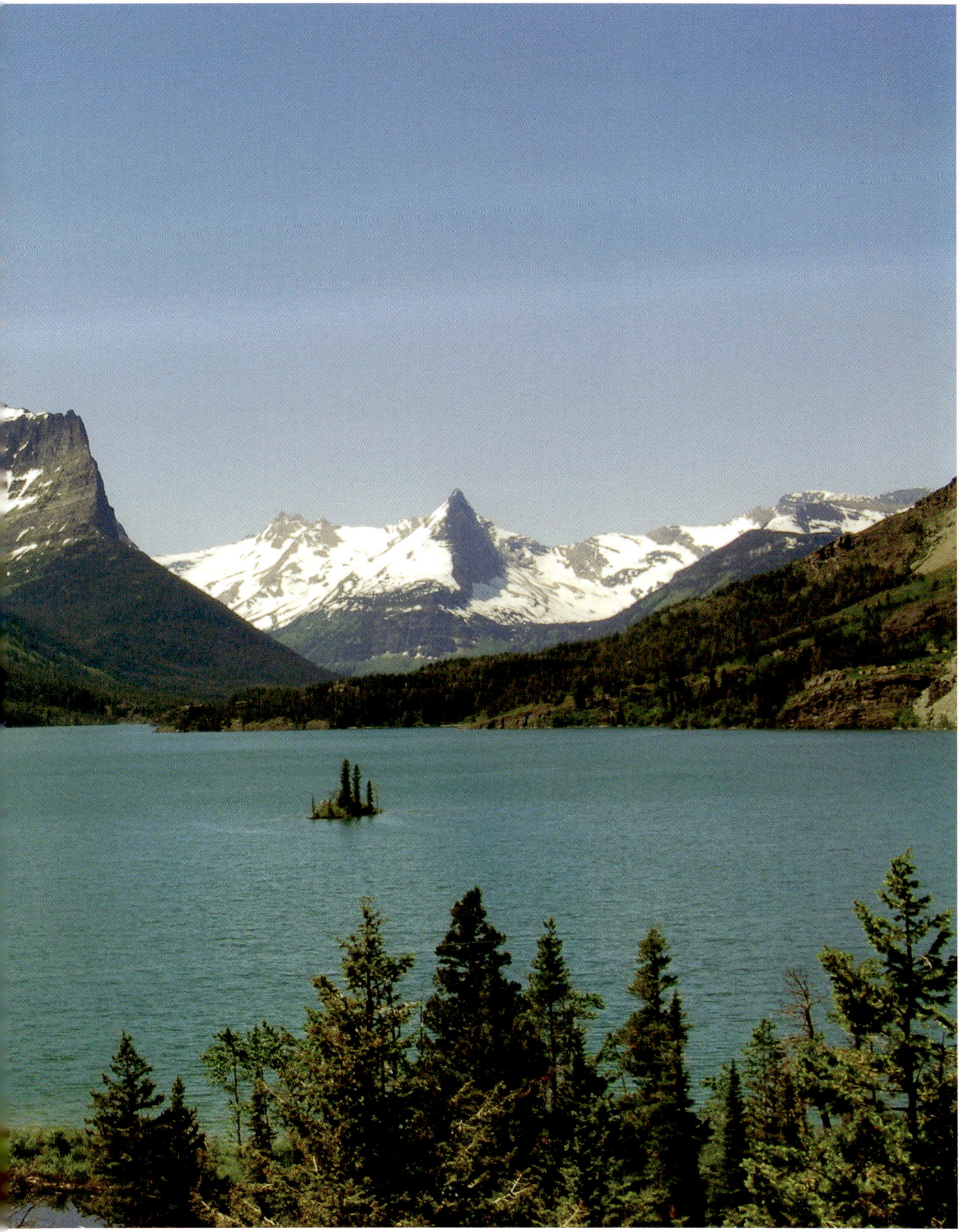

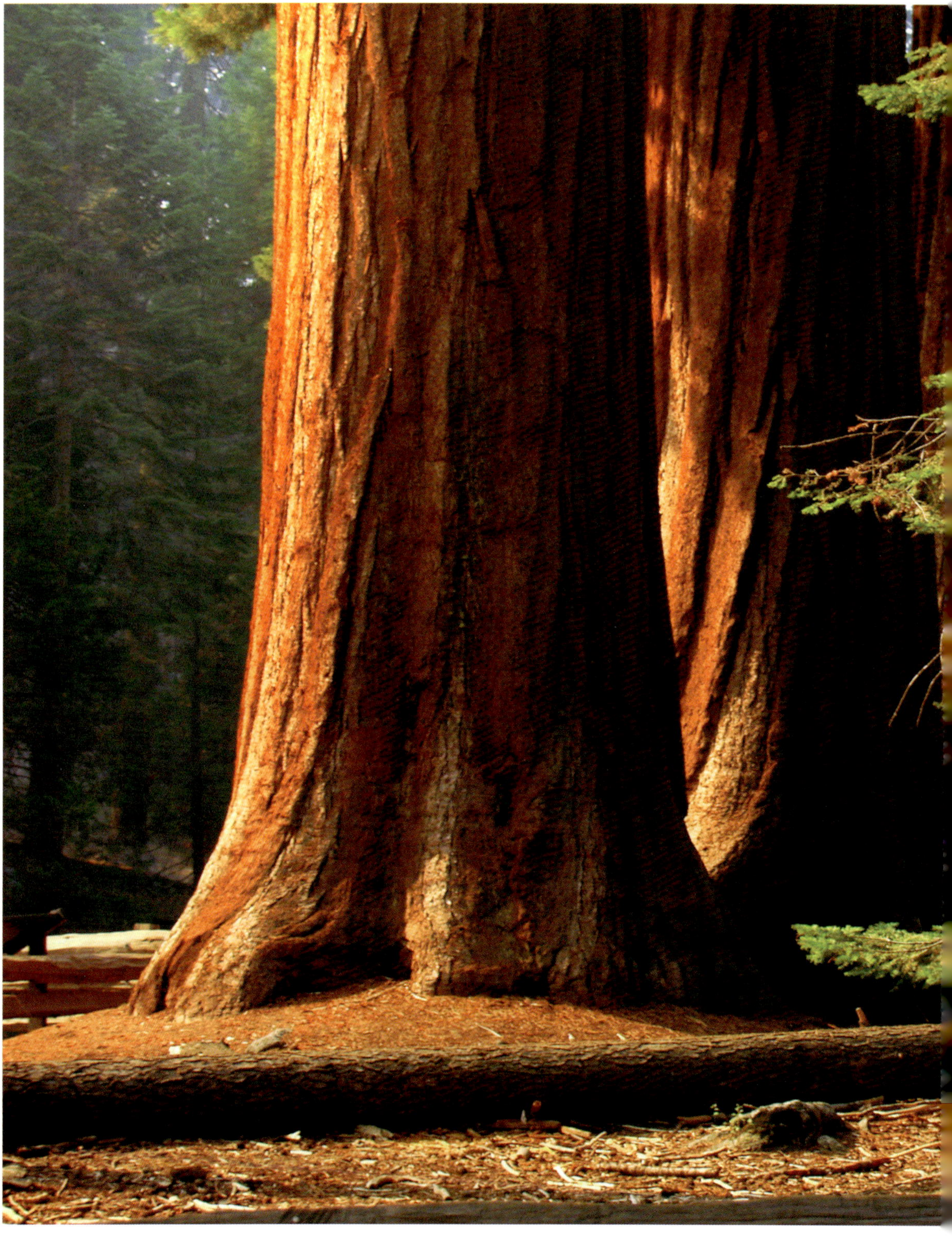

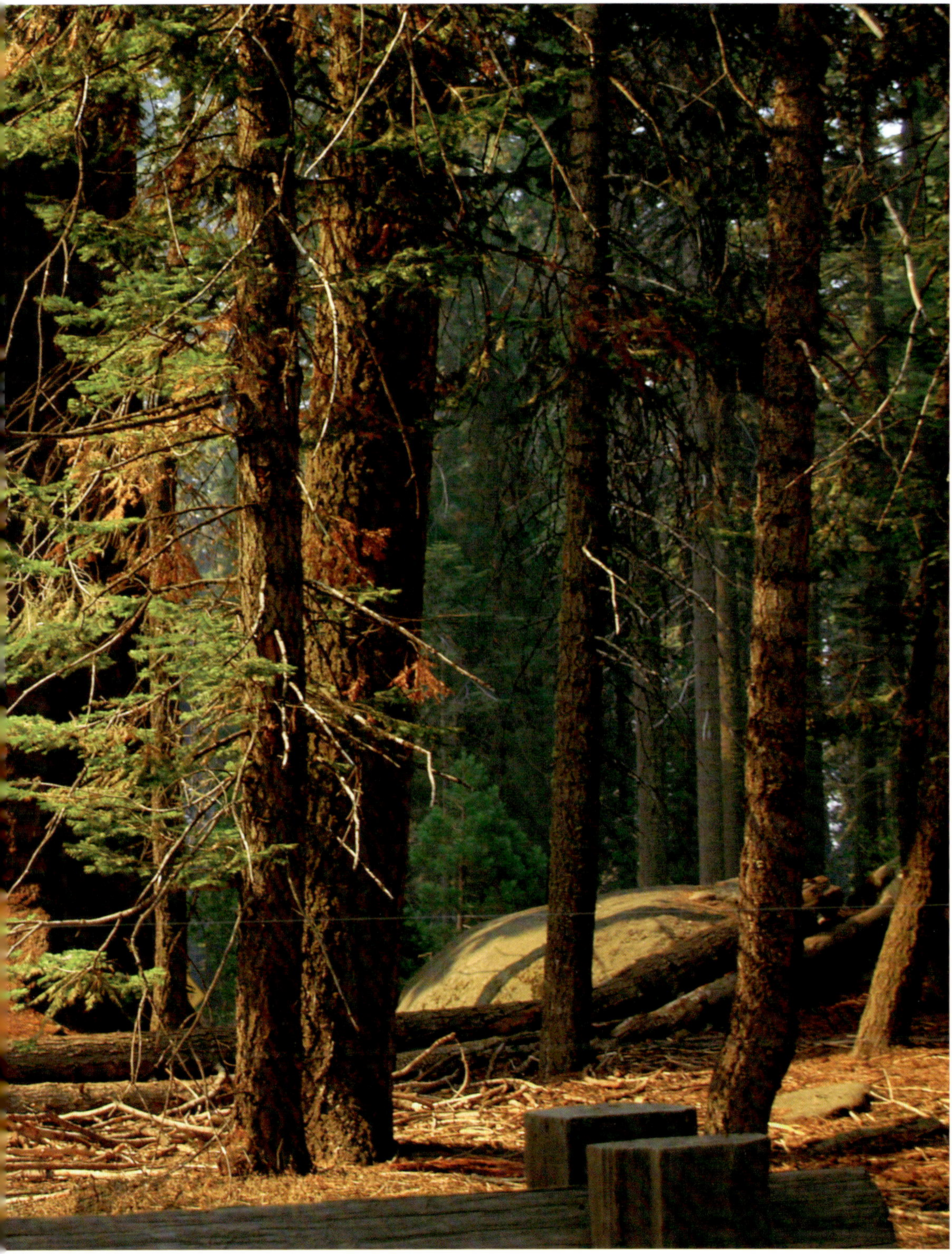

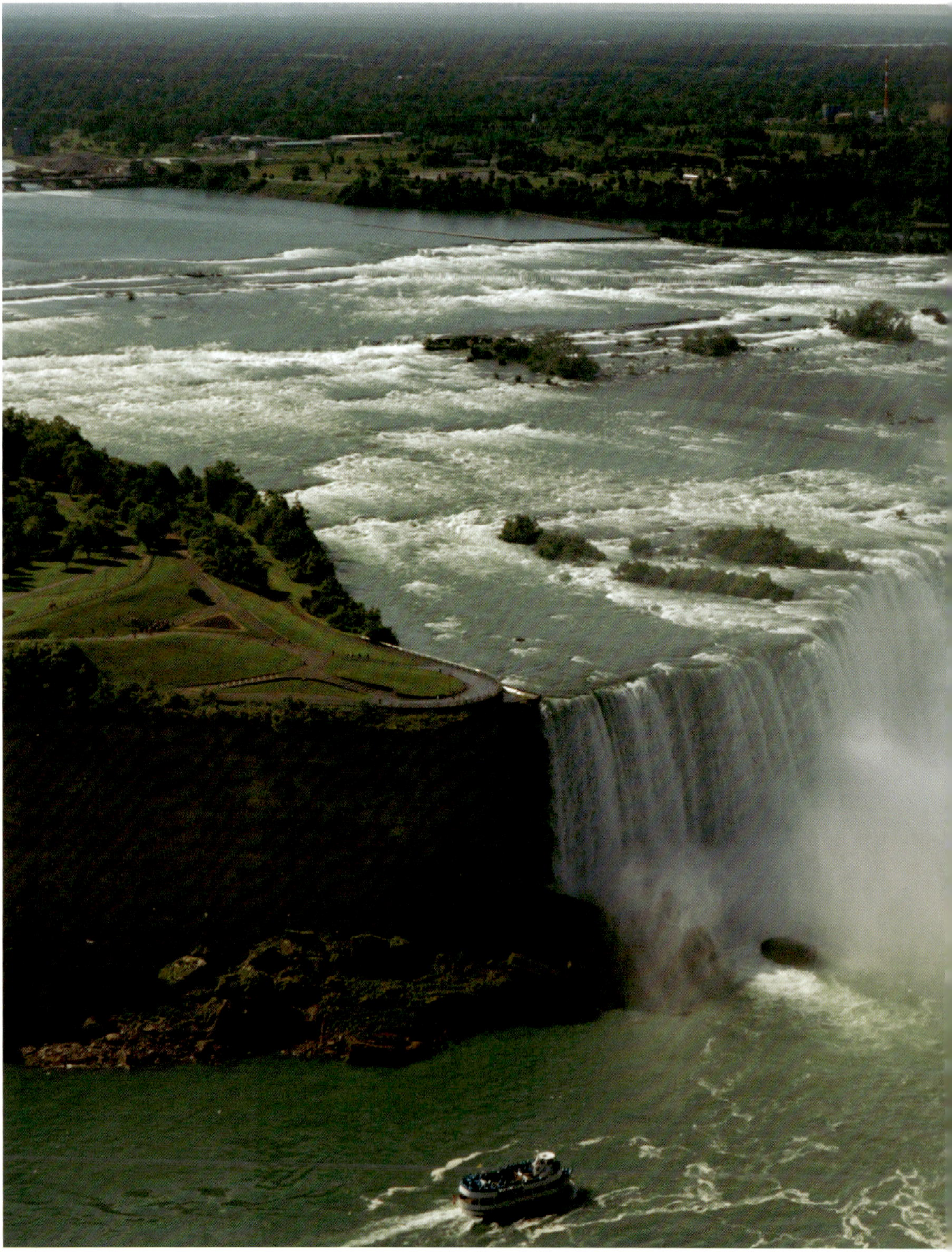

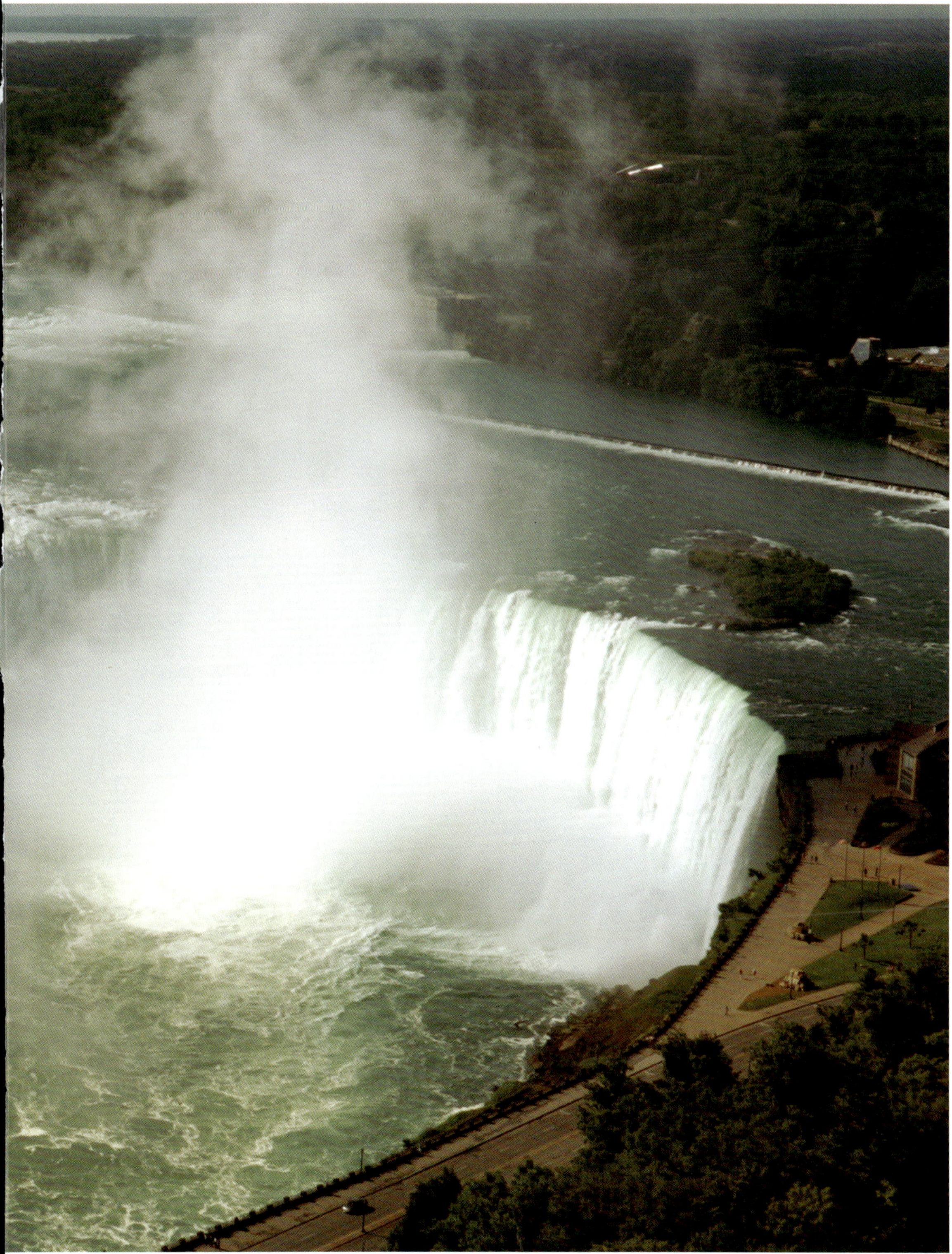

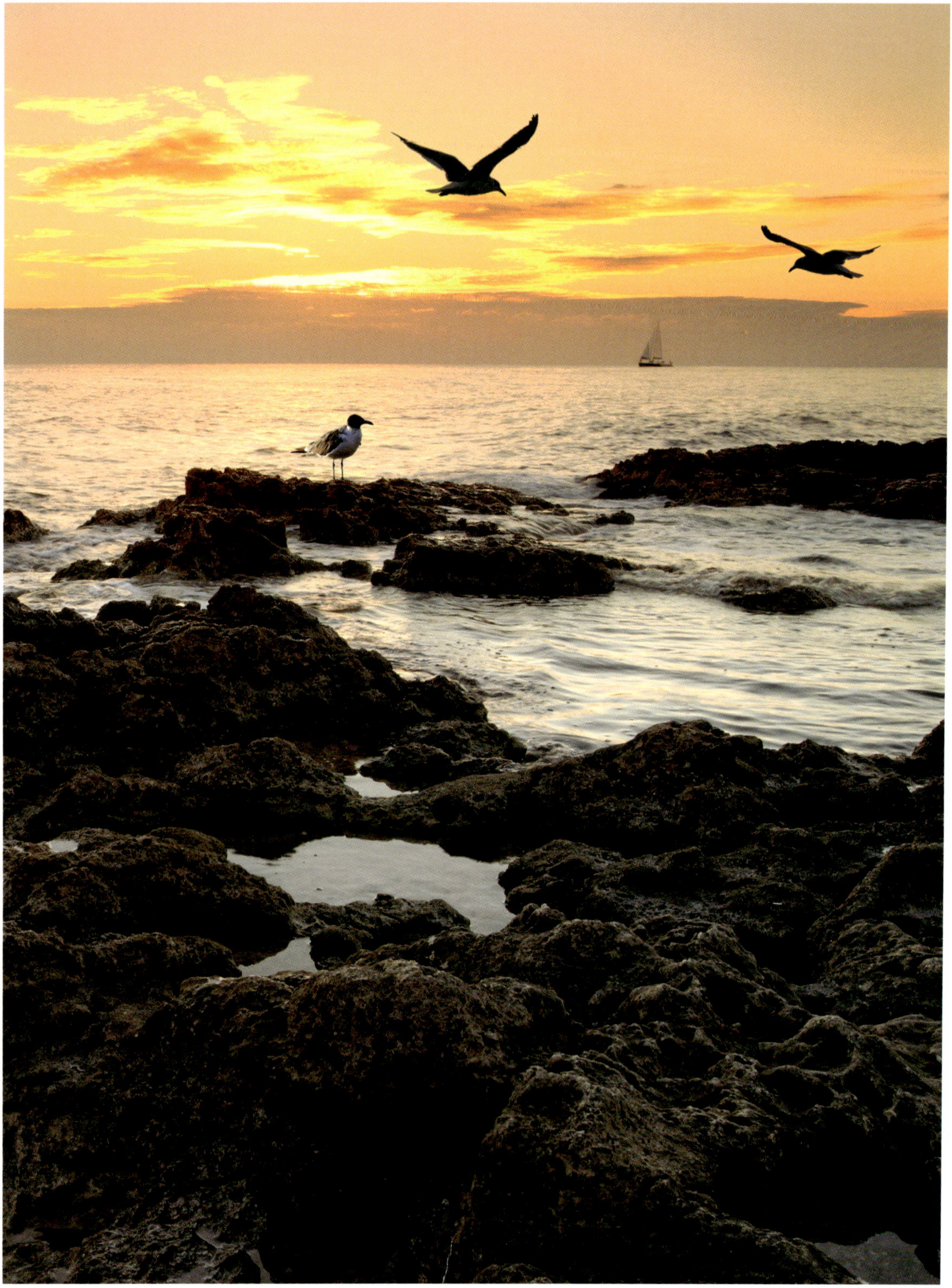